Grow Your Own Snack

John Malam

Heinemann Library
Chicago, Illinois

www.heinemannraintree.com
Visit our website to find out more information about Heinemann-Raintree books.

To order:

☎ Phone 888-454-2279
💻 Visit www.heinemannraintree.com to browse our catalog and order online.

© 2012 Heinemann Library
an imprint of Capstone Global Library, LLC
Chicago, Illinois

Edited by Daniel Nunn, Rebecca Rissman, and Sian Smith
Designed by Philippa Jenkins
Picture research by Mica Brancic
Originated by Capstone Global Library Ltd
Printed and bound in China by Leo Paper Products Ltd

15 14 13 12 11
10 9 8 7 6 5 4 3 2 1

Library of Congress Cataloging-in-Publication Data
Malam, John, 1957-
  Grow your own snack / John Malam.—1st ed.
      p. cm.—(Grow it yourself!)
  Includes bibliographical references and index.
  ISBN 978-1-4329-5107-8 (hc)—ISBN 978-1-4329-5114-6 (pb) 1. Fava bean—Planting—Juvenile literature. 2. Cooking (Beans)—Juvenile literature. I. Title.
  SB351.F3M35 2012
  641.3'5651—dc22   2010049849

Acknowledgments
The author and publisher are grateful to the following for permission to reproduce copyright material: Alamy pp. 6 (© David Hosking), 20 (© Andrew Duke), 21 (© John Hopkins); © Capstone Global Library Ltd p. 16 (Steve Mead); © Capstone Publishers pp. 13, 14, 15, 28, 29 (Karon Dubke); Corbis p. 22 (Star Ledger/© Jerry McCrea); GAP Photos pp. 11 (Flora Press), 23 (Janet Johnson); iStockphoto p. 5 (© Chris Price); Jo Stafford p. 25; © John Malam p. 8; Photolibrary pp. 7 (age fotostock/Gary Smith),10 (Garden Picture Library/Andrea Jones), 12 (Johner RF/Johner Bildbyra), 18, 19 (Garden Picture Library/Gary K Smith); Rachael Whitbread p. 17; Shutterstock pp. 4 (© Claudia Holzmann), 9 (© Marek Pawluczuk), 24 (© Bonchan), 26 (© Peter Baxter), 27 (© Rob Werfel Photography).

Background cover photograph of a close up shot of broad beans reproduced with permission of Shutterstock (© Luri). Foreground cover photograph reproduced with permission of © Capstone Publishers (Karon Dubke).

To find out about the author, visit his website: www.johnmalam.co.uk

Some words are shown in bold, **like this**. You can find out what they mean by looking in the glossary.

Contents

Safety note:
Ask an adult to help you with
the activities in this book.

What Are Broad Beans?

Broad beans are the **seeds** of the broad bean plant. The beans grow inside **pods** that grow from the **stems** of the plant.

Broad bean pods look like fingers.

Broad beans can be white or green.

Broad bean plants are easy to grow. A few weeks after the seeds have been **sown**, the plants make flowers. After that, the pods appear. When the pods are plump, they are ready to pick.

Tall and Short Plants

Broad bean plants can be tall or short. Short broad bean plants grow to about 2 feet high. Tall plants can be double this height. Both types make lots of **pods** filled with beans.

These short broad bean plants are growing in rows.

Sticks are supporting these tall broad bean plants as they grow.

Tall broad bean plants need canes or sticks to rest against. They stop the tall plants from being blown over by the wind. Short plants do not need support. They are not blown around by the wind as much.

When to Grow

Broad beans are **hardy** plants. This means they can grow when other plants cannot. If the weather is not too wet or too cold, they will grow through the winter.

A little bit of snow does not hurt broad bean plants.

These young broad bean plants are growing in spring.

Broad bean plants that have grown through the winter make their **pods** in the spring. Many gardeners prefer to **sow** their **seeds** in the spring, when the weather is warmer. These plants will make their pods in the summer.

Where to Grow

Broad bean plants are grown outside in open ground. They will grow just about anywhere. They can grow in most soils, but they don't grow well if the soil is too wet.

This is a raised bed. Broad beans will grow well here.

Broad bean plants can be grown in long rows.

The plants grow best in a sunny spot which is sheltered from the wind. They don't need much growing space, and several can be grown close together.

Get Ready to Grow!

Plant nurseries have everything you need for growing broad bean plants. Some stores and supermarkets also sell the same equipment.

Broad bean seeds are sold in packs.

To grow your own broad bean plants, you will need a pack of broad bean **seeds**. Choose a tall type for **sowing** in the spring, such as Bunyard's Exhibition.

You will also need: seed **compost**, small plant pots (about 3 inches wide), labels, garden **twine**, bamboo canes (about 3 feet high), and a watering can with a sprinkler head.

Sowing the Seeds

1. In March, fill the pots with **seed compost**.
2. Gently push the broad bean seeds about 2 inches into the compost. **Sow** one seed in each pot.

Sow the seed on its side, not flat. This stops it from **rotting**.

3. Sprinkle a little more compost over the pots to cover the seeds.

4. Label the pots with the type of broad bean you used and the date you sowed them.

5. Water the pots, then put them outside or in a warm place inside. Don't let the compost dry out!

6. If you put the pots outside, cover them with **netting**. This will stop mice from eating the seeds.

Successful Seedlings

Keep the **compost** moist, but don't overwater it or the **seeds** will **rot** away. After about ten days, the first broad bean shoots will start to appear.

Here are the first signs of a broad bean **seedling**.

stem

This seedling is about one week old.

The seedlings will grow fast. They will push up through the compost and make lots of leaves. Each seedling will have one main **stem**, and one or two side stems. Keep watering them.

Planting Out

By April or May, the plants will be about 8 inches tall. If they have been inside, they need to get ready to live outside. Put them outside in the day, then bring them inside at night.

Moving the plants inside and outside for a few days is called hardening off.

These plants have made lots of roots. They are ready to be planted out.

After a few days they will be ready to **plant out** into the ground. Put the plants into holes in the ground. Space them about 1 foot apart. Water them after planting.

Caring for Your Plants

The plants will grow quickly. To stop them being blown over by the wind, put a 3-foot bamboo cane next to each one. Tie the **stems** to the canes with garden **twine**.

Bamboo canes help to keep the plants upright.

cane

Put empty small plastic bottles on the tops of the canes. This will stop the canes from poking your eyes as you bend over the plants. The bottles make a gentle rattling noise in the breeze.

21

Watering and Weeding

Water the plants, specially in dry weather.
The best time to water them is in the morning
or evening. It is cooler then, and the soil will
not dry out too quickly.

Watering your
plants is a very
important job.

Be careful not to damage the broad bean plants when you are weeding.

Weeds can be a problem. They take water in the soil away from the broad bean plants. Pull the weeds out, or dig them up.

Lots of Flowers

In June, lots of white and purple flowers appear. The flowers make gray **pollen**. Bees visit the flowers and pollen sticks to them. The bees fly from flower to flower, moving the pollen around.

Broad bean flowers are very pretty. Bees are attracted to them.

This bee is carrying pollen from one broad bean flower to another.

After the pollen has been taken from one flower to another, the flowers turn black, dry up, and die. Then the broad bean **pods** will start to grow.

Pods to Pick

Broad bean **pods** grow at the bottom of the flowers. The pods are joined to the **stems** of the plant. Young pods look like little green fingers, pointing straight up.

Lots of pods grow on every plant. ▶

pod

stem

As the pods grow bigger, the beans inside **swell**. The pods become heavy and hang down. Pick the pods in June and July, when you can see the shape of the beans showing through.

27

Crunchy Broad Bean Snack

Ask an adult to help you with this activity.
You will need: vegetable oil, a handful of fresh broad beans taken out of their **pods**, and salt.

1. Ask an adult to heat the vegetable oil in a pan.

2. Add the broad beans to the hot oil and fry for three minutes, or until they are golden brown.
3. Remove the fried beans and drain them on a paper towel.
4. Sprinkle a little salt over the beans, then serve.

Glossary

compost loose, earthy material used for growing seeds and plants

hardy something tough. A hardy plant grows when others cannot, especially during the winter.

netting plastic net with holes in it

plant out when a plant is put into its final growing place

pod container that holds the seeds of a plant

pollen tiny powdery grains made by flowers

raised bed a growing place where the soil is raised off the ground

rot when food starts to go bad or moldy

seed part of a plant that grows into a new plant

seedling baby plant

sow to plant a seed

sown to have planted a seed

stem main branch or trunk of a plant

swell when a seed becomes big and plump

twine type of string used in gardens

Find Out More

Books to read

Grow It, Eat It. New York: Dorling Kindersley, 2008.

Websites

www.allaboutliverpool.com/allaboutallotments_Vegetables_
Broad_Beans.html

You can find lots of advice on how to grow broad beans and look after them on this Website.

www.kiddiegardens.com

This Website will give you lots of ideas on how to grow plants to eat.

www.thekidsgarden.co.uk

Discover more gardening ideas and activities on this Website.

Index